UNEXPLAINED

GHOSTS AND SPIRITS

Rupert Matthews

QED Publishing

Project Editor: Paul Manning/White-Thomson Publishing
Designer: Tim Mayer/White-Thomson Publishing
Picture Researcher: Maria Joannou

First published in the UK in 2010 by
QED Publishing
A Quarto Group Company
226 City Road
London EC1V 2TT

www.qed-publishing.co.uk

ISBN 978-1-84835-439-5

Printed and bound in China

The words in **bold** are explained
in the Glossary on page 30.

You can find the answers
to the questions asked on
these notebooks on page 31.

CONTENTS

ARE GHOSTS REAL?

For centuries, people all over the world have told stories about ghosts. Some argue that ghosts are nothing but fantasy. But others firmly believe that ghosts are real. Read this book and decide for yourself.

FACT OR FANTASY?

Many ghost stories turn out to have a simple explanation. For example, a house in the city of Bath in the UK was said to be haunted by the sound of a piano playing, until it was found that the ghostly music came from a piano two houses away. The sound had been carried by the water pipes!

 Borley Rectory in Essex was once known as the most haunted house in England.

HOAXES

Sometimes ghosts turn out to be hoaxes or tricks. More often, they are the result of hallucinations, when people see or hear things that are not really there. But not all ghost sightings can be explained away quite so easily.

INVESTIGATOR'S ESSENTIALS

Among the tools used by ghost hunters and paranormal investigators are:

Camera — to take photos and movies

Recorder — to record unusual sounds

EMF detector — to measure changes in **electro-magnetic** energy

Thermometer — to measure changes in temperature

Notebook — to record the time and place and other details of paranormal activity

Victorian photographers often claimed to have captured ghosts on film. This photograph was believed to show a man being visited by the spirit of his dead wife. It was later exposed as a fake.

GHOST HUNTERS

When a witness claims to have seen a ghost clearly and at close range, ghost hunters or paranormal investigators will sometimes interview them and try to find out more. Often they will use cameras and special equipment to gather information about the ghost. If there is no scientific explanation, they may treat the sighting as genuine.

Harry Price (1881–1948) was one of the best-known ghost hunters of his time and carried out many famous investigations of haunted houses.

THE LINCOLN GHOST

A 'classic ghost' always appears in the same place and behaves in the same way. Most classic ghosts are apparitions of people who have died some time ago. Sometimes they are even mistaken for real people.

GHOST FILE

Subject	Abraham Lincoln
Sighting	19 May 1943
Place	The White House, Washington D.C., USA
Status	UNEXPLAINED

INTO THIN AIR

During World War Two, British Prime Minister Winston Churchill was staying in the White House as a guest of the US President, Franklin D. Roosevelt. As he was dressing for dinner in the Lincoln Bedroom one evening, he became aware of a tall figure wearing a dark suit standing in the room.

Startled, Churchill said, 'You have me at a disadvantage, Sir!' The man smiled and then vanished into thin air. Churchill later identified the ghost as that of the former president, Abraham Lincoln.

The White House in Washington D.C. is the official home of the US president.

Abraham Lincoln, born in 1809, was president of the USA from 1861 until 1865, when he was assassinated during a visit to the theatre.

FACT OR FANTASY?

When Queen Wilhelmina of the Netherlands stayed at the White House in 1948, she was woken in the night by a knock on the door. On answering it, she saw Lincoln's ghost staring at her from the hallway. She fainted and woke up later to find herself lying on the floor of her room.

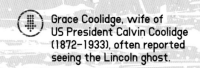

Grace Coolidge, wife of US President Calvin Coolidge (1872–1933), often reported seeing the Lincoln ghost.

WHITE HOUSE WITNESSES

Churchill was not the first or last to see the Lincoln ghost. Other witnesses included Franklin Roosevelt's wife, Eleanor, and Maureen Reagan, daughter of US President Ronald Reagan (1911–2004). The Reagans' dog apparently refused to enter the Lincoln bedroom and often stood outside the door barking.

WHAT HAPPENED NEXT?

After each sighting, the White House was thoroughly searched for intruders, but none was ever found. Since 1947, there has only been one sighting of the Lincoln ghost, but ghostly sounds are still heard in the White House to this day.

Who fainted after meeting the White House ghost?

When did President Lincoln die?

What did Winston Churchill say to the ghost?

SECRETS OF THE TOWER

Lady Jane Grey is believed to have been only 16 or 17 years old at the time of her execution.

Grim, grey and forbidding, the Tower of London is one of the most historic castles in the UK – and one of the most haunted.

THE NINE-DAY QUEEN

In its long history, the Tower of London has often been a place of cruel punishment. It was here that Lady Jane Grey was imprisoned in 1553, after ruling England for just nine days – the shortest **reign** in English history. For seven months, Jane was held captive before being executed with her husband and father on the orders of the new queen, Mary Tudor. Her ghost and that of her husband are said to have haunted the Tower ever since.

Built by William the Conqueror in 1078, the Tower of London was often used as a prison for enemies of the English king or queen.

GHOST FILE
Subject Lady Jane Grey
Sighting 12 February 1957
Place The Tower of London, UK
Status UNEXPLAINED

GHOSTS OF HISTORY

Many other historical figures are said to stalk the gloomy nooks and crannies of the Tower. The wife of Henry VIII, Anne Boleyn, who was beheaded on Tower Hill in 1536, has been seen in the Chapel. Sir Walter Raleigh, executed in 1618, is said to haunt the Bloody Tower. The white-clad figures of two small boys, said to be the murdered nephews of Richard III, have also been seen there.

FACT OR FANTASY?

One evening in 1957, two Tower of London guards saw the strange misty figure of a woman in a long dress walking on the battlements. After several paces, the figure disappeared. The sighting took place on 12 February – the exact date of the execution of Lady Jane Grey in 1554.

These two young nephews of Richard III are among the ghosts that are said to haunt the Bloody Tower.

Where was the ghost of Lady Jane Grey seen in 1957?

Who was the husband of Anne Boleyn?

Who are the two small boys who haunt the Bloody Tower?

With its echoing **flagstone** floors, gloomy corridors and gruesome exhibits, it is hard to imagine a creepier place than Old Melbourne Gaol in Australia.

The **death mask** of Ned Kelly is one of many grisly items on display at the prison.

Cries of long-dead prisoners and sounds of ghostly footsteps are said to echo down the corridors of Old Melbourne Gaol.

PRISON GHOSTS

Built in 1841, Melbourne Gaol once housed hundreds of Australia's most dangerous criminals, including the outlaw Ned Kelly, who was hanged here in 1880. Between 1841 and 1924, more than 130 prisoners were executed, and many are said to haunt the Gaol today. Whether or not the tales are true, you certainly feel a shiver when you step inside.

SHADOWY FIGURES

Since the prison was turned into a museum in 1972, there have been countless reports of ghostly figures, strange noises and glowing lights. Many visitors have also spoken of feeling a sudden mysterious chill in the atmosphere.

One ghost believed to haunt Melbourne Gaol is that of prisoner 'Lucy R', who committed suicide in 1865. Ghost hunters who spent a night in the prison on the anniversary of her death even claim to have recorded her voice crying for help from Cell 16.

When was Old Melbourne Gaol built?

Which famous outlaw was executed there in 1880?

When did the prison become a museum?

FACT OR FANTASY?

*One night, the museum's **curator** was working late in his office when he heard footsteps, followed by scratching at his door. Stepping outside, he found the corridor deserted. No wonder he prefers to work when there are people around!*

Hangings at the prison took place on this first floor landing where a trapdoor, known as the Hangman's Box, was cut into the floor.

GHOST TOWN, SOUTH AFRICA

The town of Port Elizabeth in the eastern Cape Province of South Africa is proud of its historic attractions. But inside its fine old buildings lurk a host of spooks and phantoms....

THE GHOST OF ROOM 700

In 1896, a fire broke out in the centre of Port Elizabeth and a brave local policeman died fighting the blaze. When workmen started to build the town's public library five years later, they made the mistake of removing PC Maxwell's **memorial** from the site. For years after, his angry ghost was said to haunt the building. Happily, when the memorial was returned, the ghost of Room 700 was seen no more!

Scary apparitions, doors slamming shut for no reason and books flying through the air have all been reported at Port Elizabeth's spooky public library.

FACT OR FANTASY?

One old house in Port Elizabeth is said to be haunted by the spirit of a young servant girl who was murdered by her lover. As a reward for good work, the girl was given the task of dusting the piano. People who lived there later claim to have heard ghostly music floating from the drawing room.

RESTLESS SPIRITS

Supernatural activity in a building is often linked with violent or tragic events that may have taken place there, such as murder, accidental death or suicide. Many hauntings are also said to be due to 'restless spirits' – ghosts who are sad or angry because their remains or final **resting place** have been disturbed.

BANGING DOORS

Another person said to haunt the Port Elizabeth library is its former **caretaker.** For 31 years, Robert Thomas devoted himself to looking after the building. Even today he still goes around, banging doors, stacking books – and sometimes throwing them across the room!

GHOST FILE

Subject Robert Thomas, caretaker
Sightings Several since 1943
Place Port Elizabeth Library, South Africa
Status UNEXPLAINED

The entrance of Port Elizabeth's fine Victorian public library.

Where is Port Elizabeth?

Who was the ghost of Room 700?

Whose ghost still haunts the library?

THE 'ANGELS OF MONS'

Some tales of ghosts and the supernatural seem so far-fetched, it is hard to believe that people once thought they were true. One such tale is the 'Angels of Mons'.

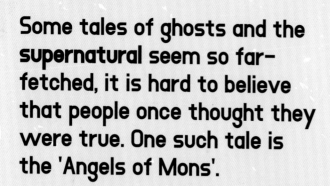

GHOST FILE

Subject	The 'Angels of Mons'
Sighting	August 1914
Place	Mons, Belgium
Status	DISPROVED

MIRACLE RESCUE

On 24 April 1915, at the height of the First World War, a bizarre story appeared in the pages of a British magazine. It described how a supernatural force of 'angels' had miraculously rescued a group of British soldiers during the battle of Mons, Belgium, in August 1914.

The story quickly spread. Suddenly everybody was talking about the 'Angels of Mons'. Not only that – according to the newspapers, even soldiers who had fought in the battle were saying the story was true!

 Soldiers who fought in the trenches during the First World War saw terrible sights that often haunted them for their rest of their lives.

BIRTH OF A LEGEND

In fact, it all began with the British writer Arthur Machen. His story 'The Bowmen', published the year before, told how British troops at Mons had been helped by ghostly English **archers** from the Battle of Agincourt, France, in 1415. The story was meant to make people feel proud and **patriotic** – but it was never based on a real event.

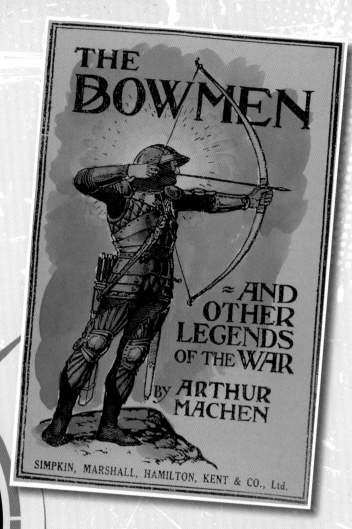

FACT OR FANTASY?

The only evidence for the 'Angels' story came from a group of Irish Guards who became lost during the battle, and were helped to safety by a woman with a lamp. There is no reason to believe the woman was a ghost, but her rescue of the soldiers may have helped to spread the 'Angels' legend.

Embarrassed by the spread of the 'Angels' **legend**, Arthur Machen always insisted his 'Bowmen' story was just a piece of **fiction**.

WHAT HAPPENED NEXT?

When Machen realised that he had started all the talk about 'angels', he was horrified. He tried to explain that his story was made up, but nobody would listen. In the end, the story was repeated so often, everybody came to believe it was true.

What battle took place in Belgium in August 1914?

When did the story of the 'Angels of Mons' first appear?

Who wrote the story 'The Bowmen'?

THE FLYING DUTCHMAN

According to legend, the ghostly ship known as the *Flying Dutchman* was doomed to sail the seas forever, bringing death and disaster to all who saw her. Amazingly, this scary story is partly based on fact.

GHOST FILE

Subject	Flying Dutchman
Date	1676
Sighting	Indian Ocean
Status	UNEXPLAINED

WILD STORIES

The real-life *Flying Dutchman* was a seventeenth-century sailing ship owned by a captain named Van der Decken. When the ship vanished in a storm off the coast of South Africa in 1676, many wild stories began to be told about her.

Some said that a dreadful crime had been committed on board. Others said that the crew had been struck down with plague. Many believed that the ship was cursed because the captain had made a pact with the Devil.

 This famous painting by William Wyllie shows sailors abandoning ship after meeting the ghostly *Flying Dutchman* on the high seas.

MYSTERY SHIP

In 1880, the future King George V of England was sailing to Sydney, Australia, on board the Royal Navy vessel, the HMS *Bacchante*. At 4 a.m. one day, the lookout spotted a glowing red sailing ship on the horizon. Mysteriously, as the ghostly ship drew nearer, it suddenly vanished into thin air.

 George V always had a love of the sea and served in the Royal Navy before becoming king of England in 1910.

FACT OR FANTASY?

Tales of ghost ships are not uncommon. According to local folklore, the Caleuche is a ghost ship which sails the seas at night around Chiloé Island, off the coast of Chile. Witnesses speak of hearing music and laughter from on board, before the beautiful ship once again disappears into the night.

WHAT HAPPENED NEXT?

Later that day, a terrible accident took place on board. The seaman who had spotted the mystery ship fell from the **rigging** and was found lying dead on the **forecastle** deck.

After this, the future King firmly believed the ghost ship seen that day was the *Flying Dutchman*. Could it be true?

When did the *Flying Dutchman* disappear?

Who was the captain of the *Flying Dutchman*?

Which British king claimed to have seen the *Flying Dutchman*?

THE GHOST GIRL OF CUCUTA

Occasionally, people invent ghosts to try to fool others. But few invented ghosts have fooled as many people as the ghost girl of Cucuta!

THE GIRL IN WHITE

In May 2007, the Colombian television station RCN showed a film about a ghost that was said to haunt the town of Cucuta in northeast Colombia. The ghost was of a 12-year-old girl who had been murdered in a local park 30 years before. The film included interviews with eyewitnesses, and even video clips showing a sinister white figure gliding through the park at night.

When the film was screened, it caused a sensation. Soon viewers started calling in to say that they had seen the ghost, too!

GHOST FILE
Subject   'Ghost girl of Cucuta'
Date   May 2007
Sighting   Villa Camila Park, Cucuta, Colombia
Status   HOAX

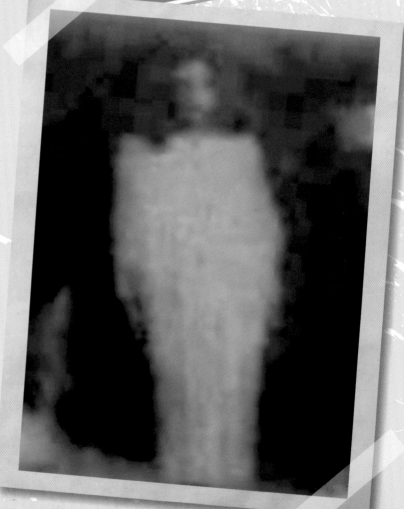

 This shot of a ghostly white figure was said to have been taken in Villa Camila Park in Cucuta.

FACT OR FANTASY?

The Cucuta 'ghost girl' hoax depended on clever visual effects and camera tricks, but also on convincing performances by the 'witnesses'. Interviews with people who claimed to have seen the ghost – including a local priest – all made the story seem more believable.

 Interviews with witnesses made the 'ghost girl' story seem very convincing.

WHAT HAPPENED NEXT?

A year later, the Colombian website trikinhuelas.com revealed the truth. The 'ghost' was a hoax created by a television news team. The interviews with 'witnesses' were faked. The 'ghost' shown in the film was a projection of a photograph of a girl taken at a **fiesta** in 2005.

Which TV channel showed the film of the 'ghost'?

In which park was the 'ghost' seen?

Which website revealed the hoax?

 This clip of the ghost gliding through the park at night looks very realistic. Would you have been fooled?

THE BELL WITCH

During the early 1800s, the 'Bell Witch' was the most famous ghost in the USA. The story of how the vengeful spirit of an old woman terrorized a Tennessee farmer and his family is among the most chilling tales of the supernatural ever told.

This picture of Betsy Bell in the grip of the poltergeist comes from one of the many books about the Bell Witch legend.

GHOST FILE

Subject	The Bell Witch
Date	1817–1820
Sighting	The Bell Farm, Tennessee, USA
Status	UNEXPLAINED

AN UNSEEN FORCE

The haunting began in 1817, when John Bell first noticed strange-looking animals around his farm. Soon afterwards, the family began to hear violent knocking, bumping and gnawing sounds around the house. At the same time, Betsy, the Bells' young daughter, found herself set upon by a terrifying invisible force, which pulled her hair, scratched, pinched and even beat her.

SUDDEN DEATH

Soon the unseen force found a voice. Claiming to be an evil witch, it threw objects at members of the family. Then it started to aim its attacks at Betsy's father, John.

On 20 December 1820, three years after the haunting began, John Bell suddenly died. A bottle of poison was found in his bedroom. The witch proudly boasted that she had caused his death.

WHAT HAPPENED NEXT?

About two months later, the haunting ceased. Since that time, many books have been written about the Bell family poltergeist. The story of the Bell Witch is still taught in Tennessee schools today.

FACT OR FANTASY?

When the Bell ghost began to speak, it claimed to be the 'witch of old Kate Batts', a respectable elderly neighbour of the Bells who lived nearby. However, Kate Batts had no grudge against the Bell family, and John Bell never believed the story. The ghost made many other claims, all equally false.

Where was John Bell's farm?

When did the haunting begin?

Who were the main victims of the haunting?

Many rural areas of Tennessee have changed little since the days of the Bell Witch. These deserted farm buildings are on the Cumberland plateau, east of Robertson County where the haunting took place.

When Sigmund Adam interviewed Anne-Marie Schneider for a job with his law firm in southern Germany in 1967, there seemed nothing unusual about her. But soon after she started work, Adam noticed a number of very odd things going on in the office...

GHOST FILE

Subject	The Rosenheim Poltergeist
Date	1967
Sighting	Rosenheim, Germany
Status	UNEXPLAINED

SILENT CALLS

First, there were the 'silent calls', when the phones would ring and nobody would be on the line. Then the lights started to flicker on and off. Calendars flew off the wall. Drawers shot out from desks. An oak chest slid across the floor of its own accord.

News of the strange events in Rosenheim soon spread. Police went to investigate, and scientists visited the office with tape recorders and cameras. But it was not until a paranormal investigator went to Rosenheim that a pattern began to emerge.

Anne-Marie Schneider was 19 years old when she went to work in Sigmund Adam's law firm in Rosenheim.

PARANORMAL ACTIVITY

The investigator noticed that the paranormal activity occurred only when Anne-Marie Schneider was working in the office – and stopped as soon as she left the building. Interviewing her, the investigator soon found that she was an unhappy young woman, who hated her job and her boss.

FACT OR FANTASY?

The case of the Rosenheim Poltergeist still divides the experts. None of the extreme events that were said to have taken place was ever captured on film. But several scientists were convinced that what they saw was genuine – and there was no obvious sign of evidence being faked.

 Sigmund Adam displays a phone bill he received at the time of the haunting. It shows that he was charged for 600 calls to the **Speaking Clock** – even though all the phones in the office were out of use at the time.

THE SPIRIT DEPARTS

Soon afterwards, Anne-Marie left – and the poltergeist left with her. But nobody could explain how a 19-year-old woman could have triggered such a storm of paranormal activity. Years later, the Rosenheim case remains one of the most bizarre and frightening of recent times.

When did the haunting begin?

How old was Anne-Marie Schneider at the time?

How did scientists try to observe the ghost?

23

THE KOLKATA POLTERGEIST

In December 2008, a young girl living in Kolkata, India, experienced a terrifying haunting. It started without warning – and ended as mysteriously as it began.

HAVOC

The Kolkata haunting took place in the house of a man called Ratan Das, just when his eldest daughter, Rima, was about to sit an important school exam.

From the 14–27 December, the poltergeist caused **havoc** in the household. Objects were moved or hidden. Members of the family were pushed and prodded by unseen forces. School books were moved, hidden and thrown about the room. In desperation, Rima's father called the police. They were as baffled as everyone else.

During the haunting, life in the family home was turned upside down and Rima found it impossible to concentrate on her studies.

24

A MYSTERY UNSOLVED

In the end no one could really explain what had happened. Was the family house triggering the paranormal activity? If so, why was the poltergeist only active when Rima was present?

Could it be that the haunting was simply linked with Rima's fears and worries about her coming exam?

DIARY OF A HAUNTING

14 December – A vase of flowers is moved.

17 December – Rima is pushed by invisible hands and her books are thrown around.

18 December – One of Rima's books bursts into flames.

20 December – Rima's bed catches fire.

21 December – Ratan Das calls the police.

22 December – Rima's bed and books are thrown down the stairs.

27 December - The haunting ends.

FACT OR FANTASY?

The Kolkata case centred around a young girl who was worried and anxious. Significantly, the attacks were often directed at the books that she was studying. On one occasion, a book she was reading even burst into flames.

GHOST FILE

Subject   The Kolkata Poltergeist
Date   December 2008
Sighting   Kolkata, India
Status   UNEXPLAINED

Where did the haunting take place?

How long did the haunting last?

Who was the main target of the poltergeist?

McCONNELL'S GHOST

Some people claim that paranormal events can be triggered when a person is in extreme danger or **distress**. Could this explain the **baffling** case of McConnell's ghost?

A DATE WITH DEATH

On the morning of 7 December 1918, Lieutenant David McConnell, an 18-year-old British pilot based at Scampton in Lincolnshire, UK, received orders to fly a small two-seater plane to an airfield in Tadcaster 100 kilometres away, returning that same afternoon.

At 11.30 a.m., McConnell said goodbye to his roommate and set off for Tadcaster. He never returned. At Tadcaster airfield, his plane crashed on landing and he was killed instantly. His wristwatch, which had been broken at the instant of the crash, read 3.25 p.m.

GHOST FILE

Subject	Lieutenant David McConnell
Date	7 December 1918
Sighting	Scampton Airfield, Lincolnshire, UK
Status	UNEXPLAINED

 First World War fighter planes were very dangerous compared to modern planes. Accidents were frequent – and often fatal.

A FAMILIAR VOICE

At the moment the plane crashed at Tadcaster, McConnell's roommate Larkin was relaxing back at base. Hearing a familiar voice, he looked up and saw the figure of McConnell standing just a few feet away.

'Hello! Back already?'

'Yes,' said the figure.

'Got there all right? Had a good trip?'

'Fine, thanks. Well, cheerio!' said the figure, and left.

WHAT HAPPENED NEXT?

When Larkin was told that McConnell had died in a crash that afternoon, he was stunned. If McConnell had died at 3.25 p.m. in Tadcaster, how could Larkin have spoken to him at exactly that time in Scampton? Had he been dreaming?

Paranormal investigators who studied the case ruled out the possibility of hoax. The mystery of David McConnell's ghost remains unexplained to this day.

FACT OR FANTASY?

A case very similar to McConnell's was reported just the year before. On 19 March 1917, a British pilot was shot down and killed over France. At the exact time of his death, he appeared to both his niece in England and to his half-sister in India.

At what time did McConnell's aircraft crash?

Who saw McConnell's apparition?

What did Larkin say to the apparition?

First World War pilots faced huge risks and were often very superstitious. But McConnell's friend Larkin was a reliable witness and had no obvious reason to make up his story.

In classic tales of the supernatural, ghosts and phantoms are often evil and threatening. But there are times when a supernatural presence can be a life-saver.

GHOST FILE

Subject — Ghost of fifteenth-century sailor
Sighting — North Atlantic Ocean
Date — 27 July 1895
Status — UNEXPLAINED

TROUBLE AHEAD

In July 1895, the lone yachtsman Joshua Slocum was on board his boat, *Spray*, somewhere off the coast of West Africa. Slocum was on his way to becoming the first man ever to sail round the world single-handed. But right now he was in trouble. After setting out from the Azores in the mid-Atlantic, he had run into fierce storms – and now he was ill with severe stomach cramps.

 Joshua Slocum (1844–1909) was a Canadian-American seaman and a well-known writer. His book *Alone Around the World* is a classic story of seafaring adventure.

THE GHOST PILOT

Abandoning the helm, Slocum crawled off to get some rest, and was soon asleep. After some time below, he was getting ready to go back on deck when he was astonished to see a tall figure at the helm, dressed in the clothes of a fifteenth-century sailor.

 Joshua Slocum's sailing boat Spray, photographed in 1898.

FACT OR FANTASY?

Most people would say that Slocum' simply imagined that he saw a ghostly sailor. Columbus was already in Slocum's thoughts, as he had read about Columbus's travels before setting out. But this does not explain how the ship stayed on course during the night.

'Señor,' the figure said, 'I mean you no harm. I am one of Columbus' crew, the pilot of the Pinta, come to aid you. Lie quiet and I will guide your ship tonight.'

Slocum did as he was told. The next day when he woke, he found that the boat was exactly on course. He later wrote, 'Columbus himself could not have held her more exactly on course. I had been in the presence of a friend and a seaman of great experience.'

Where was Slocum's boat when the incident took place?

What was wrong with Slocum at the time?

Who did the ghostly sailor claim to be?

GLOSSARY

Apparition A visible presence of a ghostly person or thing.

Archer A person who shoots with a bow and arrow.

Baffling Very hard to explain.

Caretaker A person who looks after a place or building.

Corvette A naval sailing ship with a single gun deck.

Curator A person who looks after a museum or collection.

Curse To wish harm upon a person or thing.

Death mask A wax or plaster cast of a dead person's face.

Distress When somebody is worried, upset or in trouble.

Electro-magnetic A type of energy sometimes said to be released by ghosts and poltergeists.

Fiction A story that is made up by a writer.

Fiesta A Spanish word for a type of party or carnival.

Flagstone A stone slab used for paving or flooring.

Forecastle The part of a sailing ship where the crew have their quarters.

Genuine True, real or based on fact.

Hallucination A vision or sound of something that is not really there.

Havoc Chaos and confusion.

Helmsman A person who steers a ship or sailing boat.

Hoax A deliberate trick or deception.

Intruder Someone who enters a building without permission.

Legend An old story that has often been told, but may or may not be true.

Memorial A stone or statue in memory of a person who has died.

Miracle An amazing event that cannot be explained.

Pact A deal or agreement.

Paranormal Contrary to the laws of science.

Patriotic Devoted to your country.

Poltergeist A ghost that is invisible, but can make objects move around.

Plague A disease that spreads quickly and affects many people.

Reign The length of time a king or queen rules a country.

Resting place Where a person's remains are kept after they die, e.g. a grave.

Rigging The ropes that hold up a ship's masts and sails.

Sighting When a person sees a ghostly presence.

Speaking clock A telephone service to tell people the time.

Supernatural Unable to be explained by science.

Superstitious Putting too much trust in ideas which are not based on reason.

Trapdoor A hatch cut into the floor.

ANSWERS

Page

6-7 Queen Wilhelmina of the Netherlands; 1865; 'You have me at a disadvantage, Sir!'

8-9 On the battlements of the Tower; Henry VIII; the nephews of Richard III.

10-11 1841; Ned Kelly; 1972.

12-13 South Africa; PC Maxwell; the library's former caretaker, Robert Thomas.

14-15 Mons; 24 April 1915; Arthur Machen.

16-17 1676; Van der Decken; George V.

18-19 RCN; Villa Camila Park, Cucuta; trikinhuelas.com

20-21 Adams, Tennessee; 1817; John Bell and his daughter, Betsy.

22-23 1967; 19; with tape recorders and cameras.

24-25 At the home of Ratan Das in Kolkata, India; from 14 to 27 December, 2008; Rima Das.

26-27 3.25 p.m.; McConnell's roommate, Larkin; 'Hello! Back already?'

28-29 In the north Atlantic, somewhere off the west coast of Africa; he was ill with severe stomach cramps; the pilot of Columbus's ship the Pinta.

 Victorian photographers often claimed to have captured ghosts on film. This photograph was believed to show a man being visited by the spirit of his dead wife. It was later exposed as a fake.

WEBSITES

www.ghostclub.org.uk
Website of the world's oldest paranormal investigation organization.

www.ghostvillage.com
Google's most popular paranormal site.

www.paranormaldatabase.com
A list of haunted sites across Britain.

www.paranormalreason.com
A team of ghost hunters investigate paranormal activity in Britain.

Website information is correct at time of going to press. However, the publishers cannot accept liability for any information or links found on third-party websites.

INDEX